Scotland's Railways

The Classic Photography of W. J. Verden Anderson

Scotland's Railways

The Classic Photography of W. J. Verden Anderson

A Tribute by Keith Anderson and Brian Stephenson

Ian Allan
PUBLISHING

Half title: Former Caledonian Railway Pickersgill Class 3P 4-4-0 No 54499 heads the Blair Atholl–Perth pick-up goods near Murthly in early October 1958.

Frontispiece: English Electric 'Deltic' No D9010 (55 010) *The King's Own Scottish Borderer* approaches the now abandoned Penmanshiel Tunnel with the 10.20am Aberdeen–King's Cross express in spring 1968.

Below: In June 1965 BR Standard Class 4MT 2-6-4T No 80028 arrives at Killin Junction with the branch train from Killin. The main line to Stirling goes straight ahead in front of the signalbox. Both this photograph and the previous one were taken with Bill Anderson's Linhof Press camera.

Right: One of Bill's earliest colour slides taken with his Baldina camera on 8 ASA Kodachrome film shows the Dornoch branch train soon after leaving The Mound in summer 1956 behind 0-4-4T No 55053, the last former Highland Railway engine to remain in normal service.

First published 2010

ISBN 978 0 7110 3466 2

Published by Ian Allan Publishing

an imprint of Ian Allan Publishing Ltd, Hersham, Surrey, KT12 4RG
Printed in England by Ian Allan Printing Ltd, Hersham, Surrey, KT12 4RG

Distributed in the United States of America and Canada by BookMasters Distribution Services

Visit the Ian Allan Publishing website at
www.ianallanpublishing.com

Preface

This is the third volume of photographs taken by the late W. J. V. Anderson that we have had the pleasure of putting together. The first, *Scottish Steam,* appeared in 2004 and *Diesels in Scotland* came in 2007. This book covers the entire span of his railway photography in Scotland from 1948 until his untimely death from cancer at the age of 57 in 1989.

Bill Anderson's photographs were first published in the Ian Allan magazine *Trains Illustrated* and other associated publications. It is true to say that his photographs have inspired several generations of photographers and they still do. His name continues to be held in great esteem amongst the railway photography fraternity today with photographs often being referred to as being 'in the WJVA style'.

As has been pointed out in our previous books, Bill left very little information on his photographs and we are indebted to Ian Addison, Simon Barratt, Andrew Donnelly and James Reid who have helped us to establish the locations of some photographs, the workings depicted and even the locomotive identity by studying the nameplates! Again the processing dates stamped on the slides by Messrs Kodak and Fuji has proved indispensable.

We have had enormous pleasure in putting together this third book of Bill's photographs despite the headaches caused at times due to the supply of photos being finite and the fact that we have avoided using any photos that have appeared in the previous books including the original *Steam in Scotland* pair published in 1968 and 1972. We hope you enjoy the book and the memories it evokes of times past when nearly all trains in Scotland had locomotives pulling them.

Keith Verden Anderson
Brian Stephenson

Introduction

Left: Another early slide from the Baldina camera was this photograph of 'Black Five' 4-6-0 No 44961 calling at Glenfarg station with an afternoon Perth–Edinburgh Waverley stopping train in 1956.

Below: One of Bill's earliest photographs taken with the family box camera, that used the already obsolescent 116 size film, of Thompson Class A2/2 Pacific No 60504 *Mons Meg* at Edinburgh Waverley in 1948. This locomotive had been rebuilt from one of Gresley's Class P2 2-8-2s in 1944. After this photograph Bill could only improve as a photographer!

Bill Anderson's railway photography started when he was a boarder at Rugby School far from his home in Fife, Scotland. He had joined another boy trainspotting just south of the station in the shadow of the Great Central bridge spanning the West Coast main line. While admitting he was hooked on the railway scene he quickly realised that just taking numbers was futile and that he should record the trains on film. His first attempts using the family box camera were far from successful!

The appearance of the two LMS prototype diesel-electric locomotives, Nos 10000/1, suggested to Bill that the days of steam were numbered and that he should obtain a better camera, so in 1950 he purchased second-hand a Voigtlander Bessa 120-size folding camera with a less than perfect Voigtar lens — for the then enormous sum of £10. This camera was relatively easy to carry and was to serve him through his National Service years in the RAF, during which time he made many photographic excursions by cycle from RAF Kinloss to local lines as well as taking it to the West Country.

The Voigtlander camera was not entirely satisfactory as it suffered from film buckle, the maximum shutter speed was slow and the lens caused vignetting in the corners of the negatives. So he felt that the only answer to the film problem, which was common to most 2¼in x 3¼in cameras, was to go for a camera that used glass plate negatives. By that date the only reasonably priced 2¼in x 3¼in plate-size camera made was by the British firm Newman & Guardia. So in spring 1954 Bill purchased one of these cameras with a superb Ross Xpres f3.5 lens.

To quote Bill's words, *'This was the final development of the plate camera, its design very much anticipated the single lens reflexes of today, but with the added complication that it folded. It was in*

Left: One of Bill's classic monochrome photographs taken with the Newman & Guardia plate camera of Converted 'Royal Scot' 4-6-0 No 46106 *Gordon Highlander*, with its nameplates removed, heading out of Perth at Friarton with the 4.45pm fish train to the south in June 1962. This locomotive was unique in being fitted with the BR Standard-pattern smoke deflectors.

Right: A pair of BRCW Class 26 Bo-Bos, with No 26 026 leading, have just passed Lindores Loch on the Ladybank–Newburgh line with the morning Edinburgh–Inverness train on a freezing day early in 1977. This line had a very meagre local service in steam days but after the closure of the Glenfarg line it became rather more important once the Edinburgh–Perth trains were diverted away from the Stirling route they used initially.

fact a most unsuitable camera for railway work, slow to set up, cumbersome, without an eye-level viewfinder, and last, but not least, unless recourse was made to a changing bag, always a dodgy business, the day's output was restricted to the 12 exposures in the plate holders.

'This last was an impossible imposition, and many good shots were allowed to pass unrecorded in the hope that something even better was still to come. In practice, a good day on Shap or Beattock might yield some six exposures.

'In spite of these drawbacks, the camera had a fairly reliable focal plane shutter, and the 5¾in lens was excellent, slightly longer than normal for the 2¼in x 3¼in format, and it gave a very good perspective.'

It was with this camera that so many of the photographs Bill is best remembered for were taken. The increase in quality was huge, and with quality rather than quantity being the watchword he could not fail. He used Ilford HP3 plates throughout this period that were becoming harder to obtain. However by the early 1960s the Newman & Guardia was somewhat worse for wear with only six reliable plate holders, but

replacement was delayed when Bill purchased a Minolta 35mm camera in March 1961 to replace his Baldina that had been used up till then for the relatively few colour slides taken. So there was an upsurge in colour work, particularly as Kodachrome 25 film was introduced soon after, the faster film making satisfactory shots of moving trains a possibility.

The plate camera was finally replaced for monochrome work in 1964 by a Linhof press camera with an interchangeable 120-size roll film back that was useful now that colour was coming to the fore. The camera had interchangeable lenses, an f2.8 100mm Planar and an f4.8 Sonnar. Bill said the latter, with its Compur shutter speed of 1/500 sec, was a superb lens but that the Planar was such a large lens that its shutter could only just about manage a 1/400 of a second.

Unfortunately the modern 6x7 lever rewind roll film backs for this camera had an inherent fault that reintroduced the old curse of film buckle. A lot of unsharp pictures were taken before it was realised what was wrong, and the only solution was to waste

some frames on each film. Later an old pattern 6 x 9 knob rewind roll film back was obtained. Not only was this much more consistent but gave a usefully extra wide format.

The last camera purchased by Bill for black and white work was one of the superb Pentax 6x7s in 1972. It was soon joined by a second and a variety of lenses, and was also just as happy taking medium format transparencies and colour negative film. For 35mm work he moved onto a series of Nikon SLR cameras.

We cannot help feeling that Bill would have taken to digital cameras with great enthusiasm. To be able to use much higher shutter speeds with no qualms and to have an equivalent film rating of up to some 250 times higher than Kodachrome 25 if required would have been most useful. Unfortunately the variety of trains has diminished as the quality of cameras has improved, and the railway scene in Scotland is now a pale shadow of what could still be seen as late as the 1980s. However, the glorious scenery remains and he would have made the most of it using the new technology.

Bill originally had little time for modern traction and after steam had finished in Scotland he literally retired his cameras except for occasional forays abroad to countries where steam remained such as Portugal, Spain and West Germany among others. He would take a few diesel shots just to keep his hand in and make sure the cameras were still working, but the call of the railway was always there and he gradually began taking more modern traction photographs in the 1970s. However in later years he tended to concentrate on just the lines through the Highlands, the landscape becoming almost more important than the trains.

This of course affects the scope of the material in this book. During the 1980s Bill concentrated on his local lines in Fife and that through Gleneagles, the Highland main line and West Highland lines with just a couple of visits to Beattock. He travelled the length and breadth of the UK photographing steam specials and even got down to Devon for the Great Western 150 trains. He visited many of the preserved lines and liked to make an annual visit to the Bluebell Railway in Sussex as well as the Severn Valley, North Yorkshire Moors etc. He also had holidays in France, Sweden, India, Norway and the USA, all of which had more than a little railway interest!

When writing a short autobiographical piece in 1980 for the Railway Photographic Society book *The Steam Cameraman,* not all of which was printed, Bill said he was '*still at home producing quality conventional pictures at a time when others were catching the atmosphere of the railway much more effectively with the help of a wide range of lenses on 35mm cameras*' and '*that it was really too late for a leopard to change his spots*'. We should be truly grateful that he continued to follow the style he set in the 1950s and which so many try to emulate to-day, with it has to be said, a great deal of success using digital cameras.

Left: In contrast with the previous photograph No 26 026 is seen again together with No 26 008, now in Railfreight livery, working hard on the climb from Inverkeithing to the Forth Bridge with a southbound freight train in 1987. This photograph, taken with a Pentax 6x7 on Ektachrome film, was possibly the only photo Bill took of this livery.

Below: In one of the earliest action photographs taken by Bill Anderson with his Veigtlander camera that is technically sound, Peppercorn Class A2 Pacific No 60527 *Sun Chariot* makes a fine sight as it nears Lochmuir Summit on the climb from Ladybank with an afternoon Dundee–Edinburgh Waverley express in September 1949. The coaching stock is still in the LNER varnished teak livery whilst the locomotive was repainted BR Brunswick green the previous May after 14 months in LNER apple green with 'British Railways' on its tender. Named after a racehorse owned by the National Stud that won the 1942 St Leger, Oaks and 1000 Guineas, it was the first LNER-design 4-6-2 to enter traffic after Nationalisation in January 1948, as No E527, and became 60527 in the following June.

The first decade – 1949 to 1959

The last Highland 4-6-0s

Upper left: Bill was just in time to photograph the last of the former Highland Railway 4-6-0s still in traffic. Here Cumming 'Clan Goods' class 4-6-0 No 57951, still with 'LMS' on its tender, is seen crossing the bridge over Nelson Street at the approach to the River Ness Viaduct at Inverness with a goods train from Kyle of Lochalsh in March 1951. Hawthorn Leslie built eight of these locomotives for the HR in 1918-19 and six survived to become British Railways property. However, No 57951 was condemned just two months after this photograph.

Lower left: Hawthorn Leslie also built the eight 'Clan' class 4-6-0s in 1919-21 for express passenger work over the Highland main line. Only two survived into the BR era, one for just two months and the other, No 54767 *Clan Mackinnon*, lasted until February 1950. It is seen here departing from Inverness with the afternoon train to Kyle of Lochalsh in August 1948. These two Highland 4-6-0 types owed their survival to the weight restrictions on the Kyle line which did not permit the use of Stanier 'Black Fives' on the line until the early 1950s.

Right: The penultimate 'Clan Goods' 4-6-0 to remain in service, No 57955, runs beside the Beauly Firth near Bunchrew soon after leaving Inverness with a goods train for the Fortrose branch in April 1952. It was withdrawn two months later, leaving No 57954 to work on until October the same year. The Black Isle where Fortrose is situated is seen across the Firth.

On National Service

Left: Bill Anderson was conscripted into the Royal Air Force for his National Service in 1951, serving a good bit of his time at RAF Kinloss, situated just three miles east of Forres on the former Highland Railway Inverness–Keith line. While this was not a particularly scenic area, trains did face a climb on leaving Kinloss and here we see a former Caledonian McIntosh Class 3F 0-6-0, No 57620, leaving with a Forres–Keith pick-up goods on a spring morning in 1952. The water tank at the air base can be seen on the far right in this photograph.

Above right: In another view of a train leaving Kinloss, former Caledonian McIntosh Class 2P 0-4-4T No 55178 heads a mid-day Inverness–Elgin relief conveying half a dozen cattle wagons and a goods brake van in October 1951.

Right: Pickersgill Class 3P 4-4-0 No 54481 leaves Kinloss in the Forres direction with a Keith–Inverness train in spring 1951. This locomotive was written off after being involved in a head-on accident at Gollanfield Junction, between Inverness and Forres on 9 June 1953. Note Bill's cycle leaning again the left-hand fence; he used this to reach the railway as far afield as Craigellachie and Glenfiddich during his RAF service.

On Great North of Scotland lines

Below: Heywood GNSR Class D40 4-4-0 No 62275 *Sir David Stuart* leaves Dailuaine Halt with the morning Craigellachie–Boat of Garten train in July 1955. The short branch line from the Dailuaine Distillery can be seen coming in from the right and Milepost 73 giving the distance from Aberdeen. The distillery owned an Andrew Barclay 0-4-0ST named *Dailuaine* which was permitted to run on BR tracks as far as Carron station where traffic was exchanged. The passenger service on this line ceased in October 1965, steam having been replaced by a diesel railbus in 1960, and the freight service ended in 1968.

Right: Starting in 1931, the LNER eventually transferred a total of 25 former Great Eastern Railway Class B12 4-6-0s to the Great North of Scotland section. One of the first pair to arrive, No 61502, climbs the 1 in 80 gradient from the Spey valley at Craigellachie up through Glenfiddich with the afternoon goods train for Keith on 2 May 1952. The 'B12s' replaced the GNSR 4-4-0s on the principal workings over the GNS lines, but by this date were confined to lesser duties, and all had gone by the end of 1954. Bill made several cycle rides to this location during his time at RAF Kinloss, the distance being approximately 25 miles.

BR Standards

Left: In 1954 Perth also received a pair of new Class 3MT 2-6-0s, built at Swindon for use on the local trains on the Highland. No 77008 heads the 4.10pm Perth–Blair Atholl local near Dunkeld on 15 May 1954. They did not stay long, being reallocated to Polmadie in December. In all, the ScR had 10 of these locomotives.

Below: The last new steam locomotives to reach the Scottish Region were 25 Class 4MT 2-6-0s built at Horwich and Doncaster in 1957 that included the last steam locomotives built at either of these works. Here almost new Doncaster-built No 76108, from Kittybrewster shed, enters Keith with a goods train from the east in September 1957.

Left: The first new BR Standard locomotives to be built for service in Scotland were five Class 5MT 4-6-0s built at Derby, Nos 73005-9, allocated to Perth MPD in June/July 1951. Still looking new, No 73009 tackles the long climb from Forres to Dava Summit after Dunphail on the old Highland main line with the 5.15pm Forres–Aviemore train on 13 May 1952. This line was another casualty of the October 1965 closures. The Scottish Region was eventually to receive 55 of these locomotives which became familiar on most Scottish main lines.

The Highland main line

Left: The Scottish Region had a large number of BR Standard Class 4MT 2-6-4Ts, the first 10, Nos 80000-9, arriving in 1952 but with more new locomotives and transfers the total reached 76, almost half the class, in November 1963. Here one of four allocated to Perth shed, No 80093, comes round the curve near Rothallion soon after leaving Dunkeld with the 1.18pm Blair Atholl–Perth stopping train in summer 1960, shortly before DMUs took over the service in the winter timetable.

Right: The most numerous class of locomotive seen on the Highland lines in the 1950s were the Stanier Class 5 4-6-0s. Here a typical pair of 'Black Fives', with No 44991 leading, storm north from Aviemore with a Perth–Inverness express seen on the 1 in 60 gradient beyond Carr Bridge on the climb to Slochd Summit, on 2 July 1960. Within a year their reign on the Highland main line would be over as the first Type 2 diesels took over.

Left: Pickersgill Class 3P 4-4-0 No 54486 leaves the tunnel and enters the passing loop at Kingswood with a Blair Atholl–Perth pick-up goods in October 1958. In spring 1958 Perth shed still had seven of these former Caledonian 4-4-0s on its books for working local goods and passenger trains on the Highland main line. Bill's Sunbeam Rapier car can be seen parked on the road above the locomotive's cab ready to chase the train towards Perth.

Below: Viewed in the opposite direction at the now abolished Kingswood loop, 'Black Five' 4-6-0 No 45457 re-starts a northbound goods train on a fine winter day in *c*1957 after waiting to pass a southbound train or light engine which appears to have stopped in the background. These Stanier 4-6-0s were responsible for working all the freight traffic over the Highland main line, which was perhaps surprising in view of the gradients they faced.

Kinross and Fife

Left: Ivatt LMS-design Class 4MT 2-6-0 No 43132 from Eastfield shed is seen in one of Bill's favourite and most photographed locations between Mawcarse Junction and Glenfarg with the 4.37pm Glasgow Queen Street–Perth train c1958.

Below: Class D11/2 4-4-0 No 62691 *Laird of Balmawhapple* passes colliery workings as it passes Thornton North Junction with a Dundee–Edinburgh Waverley stopping train c1952.

Right: The Gresley 'A3' Pacific that was unique for many years as the only one fitted with a Kylchap double chimney and smoke-deflectors, No 60097 *Humorist,* approaches Coaltown of Balgonie soon after leaving Thornton Junction with the 4.15pm Edinburgh Waverley–Aberdeen express in *c*1955.

East Coast freight

Left: On the East Coast main line coming south from Edinburgh, trains faced their steepest climb at Cockburnspath up the 1 in 96 gradient to the now abandoned Penmanshiel Tunnel. Here Gresley Class V2 2-6-2 No 60980 is working hard as it nears the summit of Cockburnspath Bank beyond the tunnel with a southbound Class C fitted goods that is conveying some new general utility vans (GUVs), probably built by Pressed Steel at Linwood c1959.

Right: Coming in the opposite direction trains faced much less of a gradient up to Penmanshiel Tunnel. Here Gresley Class K3 2-6-0 No 61818 from Heaton shed climbs the 1 in 200 from Reston to Grantshouse with a northbound Class E goods on 25 May 1957. Penmanshiel Tunnel had to be abandoned when part of it collapsed when the track was being lowered for gauge enhancement, and the line had to be re-routed round the hill.

On West Highland lines

Left: Running high above Loch Long with Ben Arthur, known locally as 'The Cobbler', seen across the loch, Reid NBR Class C15 4-4-2T No 67474 brings the 12.50pm Arrochar–Craigendoran push-pull train past the Glen Douglas distant signal in c1959. Two of these veteran 4-4-2Ts, built by the Yorkshire Engine Co in 1911-3 were kept for working this service until replaced by diesel railbuses in April 1960.

Right: On the Mallaig extension, Gresley Class K2 2-6-0 No 61774 *Loch Garry*, fitted with a small snowplough, climbs away from Lochailort with the 4.50pm Fort William-Mallaig train in May 1956. The first of these former Great Northern Railway 2-6-0s were sent north to Scotland in 1924, and by 1932 20 had been transferred. In 1933/4 the 13 allocated to work on the West Highland line were given the names of lochs situated near the line.

Above: On the Stirling–Oban line Drummond 'Jumbo' Class 2F 0-6-0 No 57246 crosses the River Teith in the Pass of Leny with the 4.5pm Callander–Killin school train in September 1959. As seen opposite, this train was usually worked by an 0-4-4T, but by this date maybe they were becoming scarce and the 0-6-0 had to substituted. Soon BR Standard 4MT 2-6-4Ts would take over until the line closed in 1965.

Left: Stanier 'Black Five' 4-6-0 No 45356 drifts downhill through Glen Ogle with an Oban to Glasgow Buchanan Street train in c1956. Although the line was scheduled for closure anyway, a rock fall near here on 27 September 1965 caused the immediate ending of train services between Callander and Crianlarich.

Right: With Ben Lawyers in the background, Class 2P 0-4-4T No 55263 climbs away from Killin with the 1.42pm branch train for Killin Junction in May 1960. This was one of 10 of these locomotives built to LMS order in 1925 by Nasmyth, Wilson & Co, of Patricroft, Manchester with heavy-duty buffer-beams for banking duties. In spring 1958 there were five of these McIntosh-design locomotives based at Oban for working the Killin and Balachulish branches together with station pilot duties at Oban.

The West Coast main line

Left: Stanier LMS 'Coronation' Pacific No 46236 *City of Bradford*, from Camden shed, makes a magnificent sight as it climbs Beattock near Harthope with the northbound 'Royal Scot' from Euston to Glasgow Central in *c*1956.

Right: 'Rebuilt Royal Scot' 4-6-0 No 46156 *The South Wales Borderer,* from Crewe North shed, is seen at the same location with a northbound express also in *c*1956.

Below: In 1954 Polmadie shed received BR Standard 'Britannia' Class 7MT Pacifics Nos 70050-54, the final five 'Britannia' 4-6-2s to be built and the only ones to be allocated to a Scottish depot. Here No 70051 *Firth of Forth* slowly passes the camera due to a PW speed restriction about one mile north of Beattock summit with a heavy 15 vehicle Glasgow to Liverpool/ Manchester express in June 1957. These five engines left the Scottish Region for the London Midland Region in the latter half of 1962.

Above: One can just imagine the three-cylinder roar as Stanier LMS 'Jubilee' 4-6-0 No 45739 *Ulster*, apparently unassisted by a banking engine, climbs Beattock near Greskine early in the morning with an overnight Anglo-Scottish express that includes a couple of LMS 12-wheeled sleeping cars in July 1958. This was a Leeds Holbeck locomotive from 1948 to 1964, so was unusual motive power for this route.

Right: Hughes/Fowler LMS 'Crab' 2-6-0 No 42737, from Grangemouth shed, slowly climbs Beattock near Harthope with a northbound Class 8 goods train on a beautiful spring day in April 1957. The driver appears to be looking back anxiously at the banking engine which is producing some sluggish-looking black smoke, while that from the train locomotive is clearly not showing much forward movement!

The Scottish veterans

Left: In 1958-59 the Scottish Region restored four locomotives to their pre-grouping liveries for working excursions in connection with the Glasgow Industries Fair. Two, Caledonian 4-2-2 No 123 built in 1886 and Highland 'Jones Goods' 4-6-0 No 103 built in 1894, had been stored since their withdrawal in the 1930s. Here Caley Single No 123 is backing down to the station at Callander after being turned, ready to work an excursion back to Glasgow in October 1964.

Right: No 123 is seen again as it heads the SLS-BLS Easter 'Scottish Rambler' special from Glasgow Central to Edinburgh Princes Street near Cleland, formed of the two restored Caledonian carriages on 19 April 1965. This was the last run made by No 123 before being finally retired to the Glasgow Museum of Transport.

Left: The restored Highland Railway 'Jones Goods', the first 4-6-0 built for service in the United Kingdom, heads away from Kyle of Lochalsh with the 5.40pm train to Inverness whilst being filmed for the BBC *Railway Roundabout* programme in June 1961. The small island is one of the Black Isles, while behind on the right is Scalpay and left is the Isle of Skye.

Upper right: One of the last surviving Reid NBR 'Glen' class 4-4-0s, BR No 62469, was taken out of service and restored as NBR No 256 in July 1959. Here *Glen Douglas* is seen passing Rumbling Bridge station on the Devon Valley line with an excursion train in spring 1963.

Lower right: Similarly the last Great North of Scotland 4-4-0, No 62277 *Gordon Highlander,* was restored as GNSR No 49, and is seen here heading away from Keith on the Aberdeen line with a special in spring 1962.

Left: The first diesel multiple-units began arriving in Scotland during 1956 but were relatively few in number. It was not until 1959 that new main-line diesel locomotives were delivered to the Scottish Region. Here a Dundee–Edinburgh Waverley train formed of two-car and three-car Metropolitan-Cammell units (TOPS Class 101) is seen passing St Mary's Old Parish Church at Dairsie, just south of Leuchars Junction, in summer 1961.

Below: A train made up of Gloucester Railway Carriage & Wagon Co diesel multiple-units built in 1957 (TOPS Class 100) forming a Musselburgh–Corstorphine service is seen passing Craigentinny carriage sidings making an interesting comparison with Gresley LNER Class A4 Pacific No 60024 *Kingfisher* waiting to follow with the empty stock of the 4.5pm Edinburgh Waverley–Perth train in August 1961.

The years of transition - 1959 to 1967

Right: The first main-line diesel locomotives delivered to the Scottish Region were the Birmingham Railway Carriage & Wagon Co Type 2 Bo-Bos Nos D5320-46 (TOPS Class 26) in April-November 1959, allocated to Haymarket depot. Their first express workings after running-in and driver training was on the Edinburgh to Aberdeen service. Here a pair from the earlier D5300-19 batch, with oval buffers, are watched by two young spotters as they arrive at Ladybank with an Aberdeen train in summer 1961. These 20 locomotives had been on loan to the Eastern Region at Finsbury Park but were soon transferred north to Haymarket releasing the later locomotives to start being sent to Inverness from February 1960, as they were fitted with tablet-catchers for the Highland lines.

Left: The BRCW diesels were quickly followed by a batch of the later BR/Sulzer Type 2s, Nos D5114-32, built at Derby. The first of these reached Inverness depot in April 1960. Here a pair, Nos D5116 and D5121 (24 116/21) now with small yellow warning panels, are seen with the 3.20pm Inverness–Glasgow and Edinburgh train formed of a smart uniform rake of maroon Mk 1 carriages and an SR PMV near Luncarty in August 1963.

Below: A pair of BRCW Type 2s, with No D5343 (26 043) leading, pass the Aviemore distant signal at Knockgranish as they approach with the 3.40pm Inverness–Edinburgh and Glasgow train in summer 1961. Note the old Highland Railway TPO, built in 1916, immediately behind the locomotives and which was to be withdrawn later in 1961. The later-series Class 26 could always be distinguished by their round buffers and tablet-catchers.

Enter the Sulzer-engined Type 2s

Last steam in the Highlands

Upper left: Steam continued to be used on the Oban and West Highland lines until the last of the later batch of BRCW Type 2s, Nos D5347-69 (TOPS Class 27), had been delivered in January 1962. Here on the Oban line a breakdown crane is packing up after attending to the derailment of Stanier Class 5 4-6-0 No 45400 as it was negotiating Glen Lochy passing loop with the 7.50am Glasgow–Oban train in summer 1961.

Lower left: The arrival of BR/Sulzer Type 2 Bo-Bos saw a great reduction in steam working from Inverness in spring 1961. At Dingwall, junction for the lines to Kyle of Lochalsh and Wick, 'Black Five' 4-6-0 No 45473 is shunting a BG from the 10.40am Inverness–Kyle of Lochalsh mail train in 1961.

Right: Another 'Black Five', No 45117, heads the 10.45am mail train from Kyle of Lochalsh to Inverness near Conon Bridge as it heads away from Dingwall in May 1961. These trains were the last regular steam workings on Highland lines north of Inverness, which ceased with the start of the 1961 summer timetable on 13 June.

Local freight in Fife

Left: In Fife steam still held sway on local freight workings. Gresley LNER 'J39' 0-6-0 No 64790, one of the few from this numerous class working in Scotland, comes up the siding from the Smith, Anderson Fettykil Paper Mill at Leslie before running round its train to go back to the main line at Markinch in summer 1961.

Upper right: Reid NBR Class J88 0-6-0T No 68335 approaches Markinch with a trainload of paper and board from the Tullis, Russell paper mill situated off the Leslie branch in autumn 1960. This was one of two locomotives in the class fitted with a vacuum brake for working van traffic around Markinch, most unusual for a locomotive with dumb buffers!

Lower right: Built in 1900, Holmes NBR Class J36 0-6-0 No 65323 is still hard at work 63 later years as it leaves Charlestown, on the shore of the Firth of Forth, with a goods train returning to Elbowend Junction and Dunfermline in April 1963.

The fated North British Type 2

Below: Although the North British Type 2 Bo-Bos (TOPS Class 21) were built in Glasgow, the first examples were sent south on loan to the Eastern Region; Scotland did not receive any for domestic service until February 1960, allocated to Kittybrewster depot. One of the intentions was to use them in pairs on the Glasgow–Aberdeen three-hour expresses, and a pair are seen taking the Glasgow line at Hilton Junction South as they leave Perth with the 9.30am Aberdeen–Glasgow Buchanan Street 'Saint Mungo' in late spring 1961.

Right: The NBL Type 2s proved to be horrendously unreliable, and the Scottish Region management had the brilliant idea of using Gresley 'A4' Pacifics on the Aberdeen–Glasgow service as they became surplus both in England and Scotland. No 60034 *Lord Faringdon*, transferred from the Eastern Region in October 1963 to St Margarets and then to Ferryhill (Aberdeen) in the following May, leaves Stirling with the 1.30pm Aberdeen–Glasgow three-hour express as one of the NBL Type 2s sulks on the otherwise deserted steam shed in 1965.

Enter the English Electric Type 4s

Upper left: Although the English Electric Type 4 1Co-Co1s (TOPS Class 40) worked into Scotland from both the Eastern and London Midland Regions, none was allocated to Scotland until Nos D260-6 came to Haymarket in February/March 1960. One of the second batch sent to Haymarket in autumn 1961, brand new No D360 (40 160) approaches Ladybank with the 7.30am Aberdeen–Edinburgh Waverley express.

Lower left: Another brand new EE Type 4, No D371 (40 171) from Crewe North depot, leaves Perth with the 12.20pm express to Euston early in 1962. Unlike the Scottish Region, the LMR is making full use of the train-reporting-number box on the locomotive.

Right: Another locomotive from the second batch of Type 4s, Nos D357-68, sent to Haymarket depot, No D364 (40 164) now with the small yellow warning panel, skirts the North Sea between Kirkcaldy and Kinghorn with the 17.05 Edinburgh–Aberdeen express in summer 1965.

'A1' Pacifics on Glenfarg

Left: The arrival of the EE Type 4s at Haymarket saw the five Peppercorn Class A1 4-6-2s increasingly used on lesser duties until No 60152 was transferred to St Margarets in September 1963 and then York the following September, while Nos 60159-62 were condemned in October/December 1963. Here No 60152 *Holyrood* climbs Glenfarg Bank from Bridge of Earn with the 12.5pm Perth–Edinburgh Waverley in spring 1963.

Right: A very grimy No 60159 *Bonnie Dundee* comes storming up the 1 in 75 of Glenfarg Bank with the 3.15pm Perth–Edinburgh Waverley train on a snowy March day in 1963. With less than 13 years' service it seems a complete waste for these locomotives to be withdrawn when many older Gresley Pacifics lasted far longer, but doubtless they would be due for general repairs before long, so they had to go.

The 'Deltics' arrive

Left: The Gresley Class A4 Pacifics were synonymous with the top-link duties throughout the East Coast main line, not least the 'Elizabethan' that ran non-stop between Edinburgh and King's Cross during the summer months. With the arrival of diesel traction the non-stop workings had to cease as locomotive crews could not be changed over *enroute.* The last non-stop trains ran on 9 September 1961, A4 No 60009 *Union of South Africa* working the London-bound train and No 60022 *Mallard* in the opposite direction. In this photograph we see *Union of South Africa* departing from Waverley with the southbound 'Elizabethan' during summer 1961.

Right: The first of the 3,300hp English Electric 'Deltic' Co-Cos (TOPS Class 55) arrived at Haymarket depot in February 1961 with eight of the 22-strong class being allocated to the Scottish depot. Here brand-new No D9010 (55 010) passes Portobello with the 11am Edinburgh–King's Cross in August 1961. The full 'Deltic' diagram came into force on 11 September 1961, but there were many instances of steam substituting for them in the first weeks.

Forfar

Upper left: Gresley LNER Class V2 2-6-2 No 60919, from Aberdeen Ferryhill shed, accelerates away from its stop at Forfar with the 1.30pm Aberdeen to Glasgow Buchanan Street express in spring 1962. During the early 1960s former LNER motive power became more and more common on the ex-LMS route.

Lower left: One of the handful of Fowler LMS Class 4F 0-6-0s allocated to the Scottish Region, No 44257 is caught shunting at Forfar in spring 1962. This engine has the larger size cab side numerals used by St.Rollox works. The line through Forfar, from Stanley Junction to Kinnaber Junction was closed to through traffic on 4 September 1967 with trains diverted via Dundee. It remained open for freight traffic from Perth to Forfar until 1982.

Cupar (Fife)

Right: Gresley LNER Class A3 Pacific No 60082 *Neil Gow*, from Heaton, Newcastle shed and fitted with the German style smoke deflectors, makes a rare visit to the Aberdeen-Edinburgh main line and is seen departing from Cupar (Fife) with the 1.05pm Aberdeen–Edinburgh in autumn 1962.

Left: After the demise of large steam locomotives in 1962-3, Dundee shed managed to hang on to three Peppercorn Class A2 Pacifics primarily for working fitted freights south to Millerhill. Here No 60530 *Sayajirao*, named after the Maharajah of Baroda's horse that won the 1947 St Leger at Doncaster, passes Sinclair Town with the 12.10pm Class C goods from Dundee to Millerhill in April 1965.

Above: A nicely turned-out Thompson LNER Class B1 4-6-0 No 61277 from Dundee shed comes round the curve off the single line Tay Bridge as it leaves Perth with an evening local goods train to Dundee in early spring 1963. This locomotive lasted until April 1967, almost the end of Scottish Region steam. The train is about to regain the double track and follow the River Tay to its destination.

Dundee Goods

Perth

Left: The Scottish Region originally had all the BR Standard Class 6MT 'Clan' Pacifics, but Nos 72000-4 allocated to Polmadie depot were all condemned on 29 December 1962, despite three of them having had heavy general repairs less than two years before. However Nos 72005-9, allocated to Carlisle Kingmoor shed, which had meanwhile become a London Midland Region depot, were to escape the great cull of Scottish power at the end of 1962. No 72006 *Clan Mackenzie* waits to leave Perth General with an express for the south in summer 1961.

Right: Unusually fitted with a brass adornment to its smokebox door in the style often seen in earlier days on Scottish pre-Grouping locomotives, Stanier 'Black Five' No 44979, from Perth shed, accelerates away from Perth past Friarton with an afternoon express for Glasgow Buchanan Street in summer 1962.

Above: The former Caledonian Railway and LMS shed at Perth, located at Friarton just south of the General station, was host to locomotives from a wide range of locations and in particular Carlisle and south thereof. Here Stanier LMS 'Princess Royal' Pacific No 46203 *Princess Margaret Rose,* from Carlisle Kingmoor, backs down to the turntable before taking the 9pm sleeper in June 1962.

Upper left: Well cleaned 'Black Five' 4-6-0 No 46165, still with the old BR lion and wheel crest on its tender, waits impatiently to reverse off shed and down to the station in 1961.

Lower left: Another 'Princess Royal' Pacific, No 46200 *The Princess Royal,* painted in the later BR crimson livery, is ready to work the 4.45pm fish train to the south in summer 1962. Nos 46200 and 46203 were only allocated to Kingmoor from April 1962 until withdrawal in November and October 1962 respectively.

Upper right: Pickersgill Class 3P 4-4-0 No 54463 stands beside BR Standard Class 4MT 2-6-4T No 80062 at Perth shed in 1962. The 4-4-0 was destined to be the last in its class when withdrawn at the end of 1962.

Lower right: A pair of McIntosh Class 2P 0-4-4Ts, with No 55173 nearest the camera, stand at Perth shed with Haymarket's A4 Pacific No 60027 *Merlin* and '4MT' 2-6-4T No 80092 for company in 1961.

Below: One of the five Polmadie BR Standard 'Clan' Pacifics withdrawn at the end of 1962, No 72001 *Clan Cameron,* emerges from under the coaling plant at Perth shed in 1962.

Above: Gresley Class V2 2-6-2 No 60919 is seen again working an Aberdeen–Glasgow Buchanan Street express as it heads out of Perth at Friarton in 1961. This locomotive was allocated to Ferryhill from 1945 until May 1964 when it moved to Dundee, and thanks to the abysmal performance of the NBL Type 2s, lasted until 2 September 1966 as the third-last member of its class. Perth shed was located just behind the train to the left.

Right: The 4.45pm fish train from Perth that started from Aberdeen became the regular turn for some of the larger LMS classes from Kingmoor shed in their last days, and a favourite train for Bill to photograph after work. Here 'Coronation' Pacific No 46244 *King George VI* makes a wonderful sight as it departs Perth with the fish train in spring 1962. The Scottish Region 'Coronation' 4-6-2s were all condemned between December 1962 and October 1963, but the whole class had gone by early September 1964, with the token exception of No 46257 *Sir William Stanier,* kept for a farewell special on 26 September.

Hilton Junction to Gleneagles

Upper left: The first of the Scottish BR Standard Class 5MT 4-6-0s, No 73005, takes the line to Stirling and Glasgow at Hilton Junction with a Glasgow Buchanan Street train in summer 1962.

Lower left: In the opposite direction a very grimy Kingmoor 'Coronation' Pacific No 46255 *City of Hereford* gets a clear road through Hilton Junction with the afternoon Carlisle–Perth train in summer 1962.

Right: With the Ochil Hills in the background, an unidentified Stanier 'Black Five' slows for its stop at Gleneagles with the 5pm Glasgow Buchanan Street–Dundee West train in May 1963.

Left: Stanier 'Princess Royal'-class Pacific No 46201 *Princess Elizabeth* has just passed Gleneagles with the 4.45pm fish train from Perth to the south in June 1962. Re-allocated to Carlisle Upperby in January 1962 to cover for diesel failures, *Princess Elizabeth* was withdrawn for preservation the following October.

Upper right: Standing in for a failed diesel railbus, 'Black Five' No 44722 departs Gleneagles with the 6.5pm train to Crieff in the early autumn of 1963. The service to Crieff was withdrawn from 6 July 1964 and the line lifted.

Lower right: The errant diesel railbus, Wickham car No SC79967, waits to leave Gleneagles for Crieff on an earlier occasion in 1963. Ivatt Class 2MT 2-6-0 No 46468 stands alongside with a PW engineer's train that it had just brought from Perth.

Beattock

Right: One of the later BR Standard Class 5MT 4-6-0s, No 73124 from Corkerhill shed, Glasgow climbs Beattock at Greskine banked by a 2-6-4T with a northbound Class C goods in August 1963.

Above: Rebuilt 'Royal Scot' class 4-6-0 No 46134 *The Cheshire Regiment* comes down Beattock at Harthope with the 1.50pm Glasgow Central–Carlisle stopping train in summer 1961.

Right: Stanier 'Jubilee' class 4-6-0 No 45606 *Falkland Islands* from Carnforth shed passes Beattock Summit with a northbound Glasgow holiday extra in August 1963.

Left: The London Midland Region 'Coronation' Pacifics continued to run through to Glasgow and Perth after the demise of their Scottish sisters. Here No 46244 *King George VI* climbs Beattock at Harthope with a northbound express in summer 1963.

Upper right: The English Electric Type 4 2,000hp diesels could not take the same load as a Class 8P Pacific so on occasions they had to double-head with steam. In this photograph taken just north of Beattock Summit No D310 (40 110) assists a Stanier 'Black Five' on a southbound express during the Glasgow holiday week in August 1963.

Lower right: A pair of Fairburn Class 4P 2-6-4Ts, Nos 42693 and 42192, bank a northbound express at Harthope hauled by an ailing and overloaded 'Clan' Pacific in summer 1963. The last steam working north from Carlisle took place at the end of 1967 after all Scottish steam had been withdrawn.

Towards the end of steam

Below: With the arrival of the later series of BRCW Type 2s (TOPS Class 27) they began working over the Perth–Glasgow main line as well as the Fort William and Oban lines. Here No D5355 (27 009) has just passed Blackford with an down train from Glasgow Buchanan Street in January 1964.

Right: A rare sight in 1965 was the last rebuilt 'Patriot' class 4-6-0, No 45530 *Sir Frank Ree, from* Kingmoor shed, seen approaching Dunblane with the afternoon Carlisle–Perth train. It has a diagonal yellow stripe on its cab side to denote that it was not permitted to work under the electric catenary south of Crewe.

Left: Ex-works WD 2-8-0 No 90019 passes Thornton with a short local freight in spring 1962. In the background stand the modern winding towers of Rothes coal mine, opened in 1957 and closed due to flooding in 1962. The towers were demolished in 1993.

Right: Another WD 2-8-0, No 90117, in more like their customary condition, comes round the curve at Lumphinans East Junction with a Class H goods train in June 1966. This engine survived until January 1967, and the class became extinct in Scotland the following April.

77

Left: Destined to be the last Gresley Class A3 Pacific in service, No 60052 *Prince Palatine,* with the yellow stripe indicating it was banned from working south of Crewe, stands at Dundee shed in the company of one of the last Peppercorn Class A2 4-6-2s, No 60528 *Tudor Minstrel,* in 1965. The 'A3' was withdrawn in January 1966, while the 'A2' lasted until the following June.

Right: Gresley LNER Class J38 0-6-0 No 65918 stands outside Alloa shed in summer 1966 beside NBL 225hp 0-4-0 diesel-mechanical shunter No D2717 in the summer of 1966. Some 21 of the 35 'J38s' lasted into 1966, but only two were left by the end of the year.

Left: An NBL 225hp diesel-mechanical shunter, No D2718, shunts some 16-ton mineral wagons at Alloa in August 1966. Note how someone has switched one of the engine compartment doors from the other side of the locomotive so that two BR lion and wheel crests are visible. Most of the 73 locomotives of this class were condemned in 1967, with the remainder going the following year, and so missed getting BR TOPS numbers.

Left: There must have been a shortage of motive power for Ferryhill 'Black Five' 4-6-0 No 44703 to be used on a train of coal empties, seen between Alloa and Bogside in spring 1965.

Right: 'J38' 0-6-0 No 65922 approaches Alloa with a coal train from the Devon Valley line and passes a rather smart black Triumph Herald on the same day as the photograph above in August 1966. Alloa station was closed in October 1968, but a new station has since been built on a different site.

Above: Remarkably the last two BR steam locomotives to be withdrawn in Scotland were a pair of Holmes NBR Class J36 0-6-0s, No 65288 and 65345 in June 1967. The latter is seen passing Bathgate Lower station with a coal train from a local mine to Bathgate Yard on 28 March 1965.

Right: Several of the Reid NBR Class J37 0-6-0s also lasted virtually to the end of steam. Here No 64570 passes Kilconquhar with an evening goods train from Crail in September 1965. The two full brakes are for lobster traffic from the Fife Coast fisheries which was soon to cease.

Upper left: A rather woebegone-looking 'Black Five' 4-6-0 No 45158 approaches Dundee Tay Bridge shed as it leaves the city with a train of coal empties bound for the Fife coalfield in December 1965.

Lower left: Viewed in the opposite direction on the same day in December 1965, Ivatt Class 2MT 2-6-0 No 46464 runs past the shed as 'A4' Pacific No 60034 *Lord Faringdon* reverses off shed ready to work a Glasgow train.

Right: Within days of withdrawal, Class J38 0-6-0 No 65915 stands with a train at the British Aluminium Co sidings at Burntisland in late October 1966. This company had three steam locomotives of its own for shunting the works (see pages 86-7).

After BR steam had finished

Left: A fair amount of industrial steam was still to be seen in Scotland as BR steam was coming to an end. One of the steamiest locations was the National Coal Board's Wemyss Private Railway at Methil in Fife until its closure in June 1970. Here Andrew Barclay 0-6-0T No 20 passes Methil West signalbox with a train of coal empties in *c*1967.

Upper right: Hunslet 'Austerity' 0-6-0ST No 14, built by Andrew Barclay & Co, in 1945, passes the other side of Methil West signalbox with a train of empties in 1963.

Lower right: In this photograph taken at East Wemyss an unidentified 'Austerity' 0-6-0ST reverses past the camera while WPR Andrew Barclay 0-6-0T No 19 waits in the background with a loaded coal train.

Upper left: At the British Aluminium Co, Burntisland Works, one of the three steam locomotives owned by the company, Andrew Barclay 0-4-0ST No 3, built in 1937, shunts some 16-ton mineral wagons in October 1966. A BR Clayton Type 1 (TOPS Class 17) stands with a train on the left.

Right inset: British Aluminium Co 0-4-0ST No 1, built by Peckett in 1915, pauses from its shunting as it waits for another Clayton Type 1 to pass in spring 1971.

Lower left: A second Peckett 0-4-0ST was purchased in 1921 as BAC Ltd No 2, and is seen pulling a rake of Presflo wagons used to transport alumina to the plant near Fort William.

Right: Clayton Type 1 Bo-Bo No D8612 passes the Co-op siding as it approaches Markinch with a southbound train of coal empties for Thornton Yard in 1966. The Scottish Region received the bulk of these locomotives, the first arriving in September 1962, and all were withdrawn in 1968-71, this example having less than seven years' service.

Left: The first Brush/Sulzer Type 4 2,750hp (TOPS Class 47) Co-Cos to appear in Scotland were those working through from England. Here No 1992 (47 290), still in its original two-tone green livery, from Gateshead depot (the 'D' prefix was dropped soon after steam finished in 1968) comes south past Burntisland Bay with train 1E29, the 16.20 Aberdeen-York in *c*1970. Note the fourth vehicle is a postwar LNER buffet car painted in the BR corporate livery.

Below: The first Brush Type 4s allocated to the Scottish Region were Nos D1968-76, delivered new to Haymarket depot from Crewe Works in October/November 1965. Here No 1973 (47 272) passes Craigentinny with the Cliffe (Kent)–Uddingston Blue Circle cement train in *c*1970. This locomotive was further renumbered 47 593, 47 673 and 47 790 *Galloway Princess* and is still at work with Direct Rail Services.

The Rail Blue Years

East Coast diesels

Right: On the East Coast main line north of Berwick upon Tweed, Class 47 No 47 475 from Bescot depot skirts the North Sea near Lamberton with the 14.18 York–Edinburgh formed of Mk 2 stock in August 1975.

Left: In the opposite direction to the photograph above on the same day, a rather careworn Class 55 'Deltic' No 55 015 *Tulyar* comes south with the 10.30am Aberdeen–King's Cross 'Aberdonian'.

Right: Class 40 No 40 075 heads north past Milepost 51 between Burnmouth and Ayton with the daily Haverton Hill–Leith train of ICI ammonia tanks. The locomotive carries an unrecognised headcode!

Left: Although none was allocated to Scottish depots the BR/Sulzer 1Co-Co1 'Peak' Class 45 and 46 worked regularly up to Scotland in the 1970s. Here No 46 048 waits to depart from Edinburgh Waverley with the 11.40 to King's Cross in August 1978.

Upper right: In late spring 1978 an unidentified Class 45 approaches Penmanshiel Tunnel, almost two miles north of Grantshouse with a southbound express. As already mentioned, this tunnel had to be abandoned. Part of the roof collapsed on 17 March 1979 when the floor was being lowered to allow container trains to pass, and no doubt with an eye to future electrification. A deviation was built in a deep cutting.

Lower right: Beside the North Sea near Burnmouth No 46 053 heads north with train 1S27, the 14.18 York–Edinburgh in May 1975. Class 46 differed from Class 45 in having Brush traction motors instead of Crompton Parkinson.

West Coast electrics

Upper left: Bill did not take his camera back to the West Coast main line north of Carlisle until after electrification, so sadly missed the Class 50s in particular. Here Class 87 Bo-Bo electric No 87 027 hurries past the site of Dinwoodie station with a southbound express in August 1977.

Lower left: On the same afternoon Class 86/2 Bo-Bo No 86 208 passes some superb rosebay willow-herb near Wamphray with a northbound train. Electric services officially commenced on 6 May 1974.

Right: Very soon after the start of electric services Class 85 No E3086 (85 031) heads north in the Clyde Valley near Crawford with a tank wagon train in May 1974.

Left: A Met-Cammell Class 101 DMU leads a Craven Class 106 off the Forth Bridge and approaches North Queensferry station on an evening Edinburgh–Cardenden service in July 1975.

Below: A Class 47 comes south over the Tay Bridge from Dundee and is about to pass Tay Bridge South signalbox at Wormit with the 16.38 Aberdeen–York train in July 1978.

Left: With the arrival of the HST fleet on the East Coast main line, some 'Deltics' were found to be working north from Edinburgh. Here No 55 011 *The Royal Northumberland Fusiliers* climbs from Inverkeithing to the Forth Bridge with the lunchtime Aberdeen–Edinburgh train in spring 1980.

Above: With the arrival of more HST sets they soon began working through from King's Cross to Aberdeen. Here set No 254 020 (later 43 094/5) passes Burntisland, with the British Aluminium works in the background, on the 07.30 Aberdeen–King's Cross 'Aberdonian' service in spring 1980.

Below: A Class 47 passes the site of Thornton Junction station and the still extant Thornton Station signalbox with an early morning Edinburgh–Aberdeen train in c1980. The station was closed from 6 October 1969, due mainly to mining subsidence, and the main line was realigned, the work being still in progress when this photograph was taken.

Right: The Scottish Region received a large contingent of English Electric Type 1 Bo-Bos that became Class 20. Many were to replace the unreliable Clayton Type 1 locomotives. Here a pair of Class 20s, with No 20 218 leading, arrive at the Lurgi gas plant at Westfield, Fife with a merry-go-round coal train in c1980.

Left: 'Deltic' No 55 004 *Queen's Own Highlander* approaches Ladybank station with the 09.10 Dundee–King's Cross train in August 1980. Resignalling and track realignments are taking place to improve the route taken by trains to Perth forking left onto the Newburgh line.

Above: By 1974 Eastfield and Haymarket depots had acquired quite a number of the early Class 24 locomotives from the London Midland and Eastern Regions. Here Haymarket's No 24 072 heads a heavy ECS train near Ladybank in September 1974. Most were withdrawn in 1975/6.

Left: An unidentified Class 47 accelerates away after negotiating the sharp curve just outside Ladybank station on a southbound train as passengers board a Cravens Class 106 DMU on an Edinburgh–Dundee service in October 1980.

Right: The 'Deltic'-powered 09.10 Dundee–Edinburgh train comes round the curve from Falkland Road to Lochmuir Summit, hauled by No 55 016 *Gordon Highlander* in June 1980. Withdrawn in December 1981, this was one of the six 'Deltics' saved from the cutters' torch.

Left: Possibly on the same day, an unidentified Class 40 passes Lochmuir signalbox at the summit of the climb over the backbone of Fife with an Aberdeen–Edinburgh train in June 1980. Today there is virtually no sign of the goods loop here.

Right: Another Class 40, No 40 071, is toiling up the climb from Markinch to Lochmuir Summit with the 17.00 Edinburgh–Aberdeen train in June 1976. Note the three-disc headcode being displayed by both Class 40s on this spread — perhaps the trademark of a particular driver!

Left: Class 47 No 47 525 from Gateshead depot comes sweeping round the curve at the approach to Ladybank with train 1E11, a morning Aberdeen–King's Cross express formed of a mixture of Mk 2 stock with Mk 1 restaurant and kitchen cars in autumn 1975.

Above: Another view at Ladybank sees one of the later Class 25s with the horns mounted either side of the headcode box, No 25 050, heading north on the Dundee line with an unidentified train in *c*1980. The prominent hill on the left is the East Lomond Hill and that on the right the West Lomond Hill. Both were very frequent and popular walks by Bill and his family.

Right: On the single line from Bridge of Earn to Ladybank one of the Haymarket Class 40s, No 40 168, passes the quarry at Newburgh with an Inverness–Edinburgh train in *c*1975. The River Tay can be seen in the background.

Left: Newburgh Quarry was rail-connected and supplied ballast to British Rail, and was probably the reason this line survived, which was lucky as after the closure of the Glenfarg route it soon became clear that routing Edinburgh–Perth trains via Stirling was not working well. Here BRCW Class 26 No 26 021 approaches the entrance to the quarry in September 1975.

Right: Viewed in the opposite direction towards Lindores, Class 20 No 20 201, a Tinsley locomotive, shunts a train of ballast that has just been brought out of the quarry in 1975.

Above: With the River Tay in the background on a June evening in 1977 a pair of Class 26 Bo-Bos pass the entrance to Newburgh Quarry with the 16.30 Inverness–Edinburgh train.

Upper right: Very late on a June evening near Kingskettle the sun is still quite high as a Class 27 takes a cement train north, bound for Craiginches Cement Terminal in Aberdeen.

Lower right: The sun is setting behind the Lomond Hill as a Class 24/25 and a '47' head south between Ladybank and Kingskettle with the 16.20 Aberdeen–York train in late February 1971.

Below: Late-series Class 24 No 5120 (24 120), fitted with headlights for the Highland lines, heads away from Perth near Seggreden, on the north bank of the River Tay which is on the left, with a van train for Dundee in *c*1972.

Right: Probably on the same working from Perth to Dundee, a Class 40 is seen within a mile of the same location but from the other side of the River Tay. Note the ex-works two-car Met-Cammell Class 101 DMU in the consist.

Above: HST set No 254 017 (43 088/9) passes Montrose South signalbox with the Montrose Basin in the background as it heads away from Montrose and enters the single line section to Usan on an Aberdeen–King's Cross service in late September 1980.

Right: Class 47 No 47 708 *Waverley* propels an Aberdeen–Edinburgh train over the River Esk Viaduct as it accelerates up the hill out of Montrose in September 1983.

The Highland main line

Above: A solitary Inverness Class 24 passes the heather-covered moorland halfway up the climb from Carrbridge to Slochd Summit in *c*1976 with the 06.30 Perth–Inverness train that conveyed a travelling post office. Note the restaurant car between a full brake and the TPO. Until November 1967 the TPO would be transferred at Inverness to the 10.40 Wick train as far as Helmsdale, then from 7 October 1978 ceased altogether.

Left: In April 1971 a Class 26 and Class 24 are working at full throttle as they power their heavy 15-carriage train, the up 'Royal Highlander', with sleeper accommodation and TPO, up the final mile to Druimuachdar Summit in the rain beside the A9 road where some dangerous overtaking seems to be taking place. Note the leading locomotive's cab door has been swapped from a green locomotive and also the fact that tablet catchers have been dispensed with by this date.

Right: An early-series Class 24 and a Class 26 pass straight through the loop at Dalnacardoch as they speed downhill from Druimuachdar Summit past a glorious bank of heather with the 15-vehicle 19.30 Inverness–Euston 'Royal Highlander' in the early 1970s. This section of track was formerly double-track and has since been re-doubled.

Left: A very hard-working Class 40 No 40 058 passes the former passing loop signalbox at Dalnacardoch on the climb to Druimuachdar Summit with the overnight sleeping car train from Euston, the 'Royal Highlander', early on a September morning in 1979. When this section of track was re-doubled the signalbox was retained as a ground frame to work an emergency crossover. Ben Vrackie is the peak in the centre of the photograph, and below to the left construction of the new A9 road can be seen.

Upper right: A pair of Class 24s with No 5127 leading as they pass Milepost 79½ crossing the Moor of Alvie, between Aviemore and Kincraig, with an Inverness–Glasgow/Edinburgh train *c*1970.

Lower right: The pioneer Class 47 No 47 401 *North Eastern* (D1500) is working hard as it climbs the 1 in 70 to Druimuachdar in Glen Garry to the north of Struan with the heavily laden 'Clansman' from King's Cross to Inverness in late summer 1983.

Left: No book on Scottish railways would be complete without a view of Killiekrankie Viaduct! Here a pair of Class 26s leave the tunnel soon after passing the closed station and cross the viaduct with the 12.30 Inverness–Glasgow Queen Street in early spring 1980.

Right: A Class 47 is seen through the trees in the narrow valley of the River Garry from high above the tunnel as it crosses Killiekrankie Viaduct with the 13.22 Edinburgh to Inverness later on the same day in spring 1980.

Left: Gateshead Class 47 No 47 421 *The Brontes of Haworth* crosses the River Garry near Edendon with the 13.22 Edinburgh–Inverness in July 1986. The new A9 road can be seen above the train where the dual carriageway runs at two levels.

Above: In Strath Tay Class 47 No 47 469 *Glasgow Chamber of Commerce* arrives at Dunkeld with the summer-only 14.30 Inverness–Glasgow Queen Street during September 1983. Note the tall signal so that it could be seen from round the bend past the end of the train.

Left: Seen from high on Tulach Hill In February 1987 with Blair Castle in the left-hand background, Class 47 No 47 460, sporting large-logo livery, approaches Blair Atholl station with a southbound train from Inverness. The snow-capped peak is Meall Reamhar.

Right: Another large-logo-liveried Class 47, No 47 439, crosses the bridge over the River Tilt as it approaches Blair Atholl at around the same date from the south with an Inverness train. The Ben A'Ghio range of hills are in the background.

The West Highlands

Above: A grubby unidentified Class 27 crosses one of the steel bridges that abound on the West Highland line at Achallader, on the climb from Bridge of Orchy to Rannoch, with the morning train from Fort William to Glasgow in August 1978. Loch Tulla can just be glimpsed to the right.

Right: The Fort William–Euston sleeping car train is seen at the County March summit after negotiating the horseshoe curve between Bridge of Orchy and Tyndrum Upper in *c*1984 hauled by a single Class 37 Co-Co and an 'Ethel' — a Class 25 utilised solely to supply electric power to heat the train.

Left: The 1,000hp English Electric Class 20 Bo-Bos could occasionally be found working freight trains in pairs on the West Highland line. Here an unidentified pair are seen coming downgrade from Tyndrum Upper towards Crianlarich at Inverhaggernie in Strath Fillan with an up freight in March 1978.

Left: Class 27 No 27 037 has just negotiated the horseshoe curve between Bridge of Orchy and Tyndrum Upper with a trainload of timber going south in April 1979. The peak of Ben Mhanach can be seen on the left while Ben Odhar rises to the right.

Right: The first Class 37s arrived in the West Highlands during January 1978 and were to take an ever increasing share of the duties to Fort William and Oban. Here No 37 011 draws into Crianlarich Upper with a fuel oil train, possibly for Connel Ferry, in March 1985.

Below: Seen near Achallader early in 1986 a pair of Class 37s in large-logo livery, Nos 37 423 and 37 401 *Mary Queen of Scots,* go south with a train of empty alumina wagons from Fort William. The first Class 37/4s fitted with electric train heating (ETH) reached Scotland in June 1984.

Right: The penultimate Scotish ETH Class 37/4, No 37 424, tows 97 250 *Ethel 1*, heading north out of Crianlarich bound for Fort William in March 1986. By this date the former locomotive would only be used for heating the sleepers before the train engine was available to couple up and supply power.

Left: On the Oban line, Class 27 No 27 021 heads away from Connel Ferry with the lunchtime Oban–Glasgow Queen Street in May 1977. The cantilevered bridge in the background once carried the Ballachulish branch which it shared with the A828 road to that town across the Falls of Lora, where the seawater Loch Etive can be seen racing through to the sea on the ebb tide.

Upper right: Ex-works Class 27 No 27 021 climbs up Glen Lochy from Dalmally to the 840ft summit just short of Tyndrum Lower with the lunchtime Oban–Glasgow in *c*1976. Ben Cruachan is in the background.

Lower right: In the opposite direction the lunchtime Glasgow–Oban is approaching Tyndrum Lower behind an unidentified Class 27 in March 1980.

Left: Class 27 No 27 005 heads away from Crianlarich towards Tyndrum Lower with the lunchtime Glasgow–Oban on a snowy March day in 1978. Ben More and Stob Binnein are the two peaks in the distance.

Left: The morning Fort William–Glasgow train is seen crossing the Auchtertyre Viaduct between Tyndrum Upper and Crianlarich with its Class 27 nicely placed against the snow on the slopes of Beinn Chaorach in early spring 1973.

Right: Also in March 1978 a Class 25 Bo-Bo pilots Class 27 No 27 029 as they depart from Crianlarich with a Glasgow train.

Left: The first Class 37 to be transferred to the West Highland line back in 1978, No 37 108 is seen happily working on the Oban line on a glorious day in August 1984 with the 12.25 Oban–Glasgow. It is pulling away from the request stop at Tyndrum Lower. The prominent hill in the background is Ben Dorainwhich and is passed by the Fort William line, out of view behind the trees, as is Tyndrum Upper station.

Below: Judging by the heads out of the carriage windows the passengers are enjoying a good thrash from No 37 022 as it climbs the short 1 in 49 climb out of Tyndrum Lower to the 840ft summit with the 12.55 Glasgow–Oban earlier on the same day in August 1984. Tyndrum Upper station can be seen above the third coach; co-author Keith apologises for getting in his father's photograph as he stands high up on the right!

Left: On the Mallaig Extension, the final Scottish Class 37/4, No 37 425 *Sir Robert McAlpine/Concrete Bob,* in large-logo livery with the Eastfield West Highland Terrier logo on its bodyside, has just climbed the 1 in 50 gradient from Loch Eilt in the background and is about to enter the first of the two short Leachabhuidh Tunnels before reaching the summit of the line and descending to Glenfinnan station with a Mallaig–Fort William train in April 1988.

Right: In the opposite direction No 37 408 *Loch Rannoch* skirts the end of Loch Eilt with a Fort William–Mallaig train in July 1988. This was one of the last photographs taken in the West Highlands by Bill, using Fujichrome slide film.

Upper left: With the Ben Nevis range in the background, No 37 404 *Ben Cruachan* crosses the River Spean on another of the steel bridges on the West Highland line as it slows for its stop at Tulloch with the overnight sleeper from Euston to Fort William in June 1988.

Lower left: No 37 404 *Ben Cruachan* is seen a second time as it erupts into motion after a brief stop at Tyndrum Upper with the 14.45 Fort William–Glasgow in late summer 1987.

Right: On a July morning in 1988, No 37 424 *Isle of Mull* passes the dammed end of Loch Treig between Tulloch and Corrour with the 08.40 Fort William–Glasgow train shortly after the northbound sleeper had passed in the opposite direction. 'Sprinter' DMUs took over most of these services from 23 January the following year.

Left: Amid superb autumn tints, Class 47 No 47 586 is about to pass under the A9 road north of Dunkeld with the up 'Clansman', the 10.30 Inverness–Euston, in November 1987. This locomotive only ever received a half-baked attempt by Inverness depot at putting it into the large-logo livery, and it went straight from this into the InterCity 'Swallow' scheme.

Below: With the Highland Rail stag logo on its cab side, large-logo-liveried No 47 614 crosses the River Tilt as it approaches Blair Atholl with an afternoon train for Inverness in late October 1985. Ben Vrackie is prominent in the background. This was originally the XP64-liveried No D1733 and survives to this day as No 47 853 working for Direct Rail Services.

Large-logo livery on the Highland main line

Upper left: Large-logo Class 37 No 37 153 from Inverness depot heads south past Milepost 22 between Dalguise and Ballinluig with a mixed freight early in 1989.

Lower left: Class 37s were relatively rare on passenger trains over the Highland main line. Here No 37 412 *Loch Lomond,* one of the Eastfield allocation of 17 '37/4s', heads north between Dalguise and Ballinluig, having just crossed the bridge over the River Tay with a train for Inverness in winter 1988-9.

Right: Early in 1989 No 37 418 *An Comunn Gaidhealach,* one of the eight Inverness-based Class 37/4s, comes hurtling south down Druimuachdar leaving a wake of powdered snow, having just come round the curve from the closed Dalnaspidal station with a train bound for Edinburgh or Glasgow.

Left: Class 47 No 47 593 *Galloway Princess* faces the short but steep climb to Slochd Summit (between 1 in 60/70 for the next five miles) as it restarts from Carrbridge station with an Inverness train late in 1985. Bill had chased this train all the way up from Ballinluig and this was the fifth good photograph he managed to take of it. This locomotive remains at work today with Direct Rail Services and has been renamed *Galloway Princess* having carried the name *Saint David/Dewi Sant* for a time. It was entering the loop here that a Stobart-liveried Class 66 was derailed when its train ran away down Slochd on 4 January 2010.

Above: With most of its train formed of Mk 3 stock in InterCity Executive livery, No 47 629 heads south down Druimuachdar Pass, just north of Calvine on the re-doubled section to Blair Atholl, hauling the Inverness–Euston 'Clansman' service early in 1987. This locomotive, previously numbered 47 266, became 47 828, and went to Virgin Trains on privatisation and was named *Severn Valley Railway*. In 2005 it was sold to Cotswold Rail and was renamed *Joe Strummer*; it is currently stored at Doncaster after the collapse of this company, awaiting possible new owners and reactivation.

149

Left: Class 47 No 47 563 *Women's Guild* passes a field flooded by the River Tay between Dunkeld and Dalguise as it heads north with a train for Inverness early in 1989. This locomotive was rebuilt as a Class 57/3 for Virgin Trains by Brush Traction, becoming 'Thunderbird' No 57 310 *Kyrano* in July 2003.

Below: Immediately after being named *Women's Royal Voluntary Service* on 3 August 1988, No 47 604 passes Dalwhinnie with the 'Royal Scotsman' bound for Aviemore. It later became 47 854 and now works for the West Coast Railway Co which also now operates this train.

InterCity and ScotRail

Upper left: Painted in ScotRail InterCity livery, No 47 643 speeds north alongside Loch Insh on the fast section between Kingussie and Kincraig loop in the summer of 1986. The white house on the far side of the loch belongs to Bill's brother David, while a little further to the right in the trees was the home of his sister Helen. Bill seriously considered buying the station at Kincraig after it closed, but to the author's dismay his mother Birgitta understandably would not agree! The locomotive is preserved by the SRPS at Bo'ness.

Lower left: Seen from the road bridge near the old signalbox at Dalnacardoch, InterCity-liveried No 47 549 *Royal Mail* from Old Oak Common depot hurries down from Druimuachdar with the up 'Clansman', the 10.30 Inverness–Euston, in autumn 1986.

Right: One of the few Class 37s painted in InterCity colours but without branding — so called Mainline livery, No 37 401 *Mary Queen of Scots* runs high above Loch Tulla, near Achallader between Bridge of Orchy and Rannoch on the West Highland line, with a northbound engineers' train *c*1988. At the time of writing this locomotive is still operational with EWS/DB Schenker, but possibly not for much longer.

Left: In ScotRail InterCity livery No 47 492 *The Enterprising Scot* from Inverness depot heads north beside the A9 road near Ballinluig with the early morning Edinburgh–Inverness in autumn 1987. This locomotive is now privately preserved.

Below: In the earlier IC125 livery, HST power car No 43 194 *Royal Signals* leads the southbound 'Clansman' from Inverness to King's Cross south of Perth between Forteviot and Gleneagles on a beautiful autumn morning in 1987.

Left: One of the push/pull Class 47/7s, No 47 708 *Waverley,* in the ScotRail blue stripe livery, hauls a Glasgow Queen Street–Edinburgh train between Croy and Falkirk Upper stations, near to the Castlecary Viaduct, in spring 1987.

Upper right: Under a dramatic sky Class 47/7 No 47 708 *Waverley* is seen again as it propels a shortened Mk 3 push/pull set towards Plean Junction on 13 April 1985. It had spent the day working a shuttle service between Perth and Perth Freight Yard as part of the Perth Rail Fair.

Lower right: No 47 711 *Greyfriars Bobby* propels a push/pull set towards the Calton Hill Tunnel and Edinburgh Waverley station with an empty stock working from Craigentinny in December 1987.

The Freight Sector liveries

Above: Sadly Bill Anderson did not live long enough to see many locomotives repainted into the various freight sector liveries. One of the half dozen or so he did photograph was Class 47 No 47 144, in Railfreight Distribution livery, seen here descending Druimuachdar between Dalnacardoch and Calvine with an afternoon southbound mixed freight in March 1989.

Right: In one of Bill's last photographs Class 37/4 No 37 423 *Sir Murray Morrison 1873-1948 Pioneer of British Aluminium Industry,* in Trainload Freight Metals livery, is fairly unusually seen on a northbound passenger train for Inverness passing the site of Struan station near Calvine in June 1989. Ben Vrackie is seen again over on the far left.

Index of locations

Index of locomotive classes